Ace Academic Publishing
ACHIEVING EXCELLENCE TOGETHER

LEARN THE ALPHABET WITH DINOSAURS

www.aceacademicprep.com

Author: Ace Academic Publishing

Ace Academic Publishing is a leading supplemental educational workbook publisher for grades K-12. At Ace Academic Publishing, we realize the importance of imparting analytical and critical thinking skills during the early ages of childhood and hence our books include materials that require multiple levels of analysis and encourage the students to think outside the box.

The materials for our books are written by award winning teachers with several years of teaching experience. All our books are aligned with state standards and are widely used by many schools throughout the country.

For enquiries and bulk order, contact us at the following address:

3736, Fallon Road, #403
Dublin, CA 94568
www.aceacademicprep.com

Ace Academic Publishing
ACHIEVING EXCELLENCE TOGETHER

ISBN: 978-1-949383-16-4

Parent's Guide

Use this book to introduce the alphabet
to your child while learning fun dinosaur facts.
The activities in the book will keep your child
engaged and will also be fun to play.

Ace Academic Publishing
ACHIEVING EXCELLENCE TOGETHER

Other books from Ace Academic Publishing

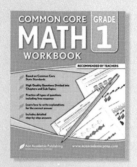
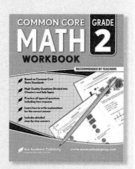
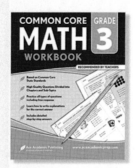
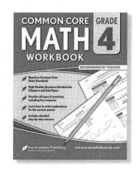

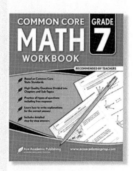
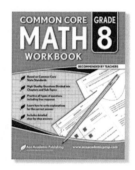

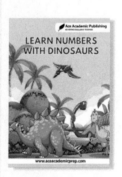

Ace Academic Publishing
ACHIEVING EXCELLENCE TOGETHER

DINOSAURS

HELLO EVERYONE!
WE ARE THE DINOSAUR FAMILY AND WE ARE
EXCITED TO LEARN THE ALPHABET WITH YOU!

DID YOU ASK, "WHO ARE DINOSAURS?"

OK THEN, WE WILL SHARE A LOT OF FUN FACTS ABOUT
OUR FAMILY WHILE LEARNING THE ALPHABET WITH YOU!

ARE YOU READY? LET'S GO!

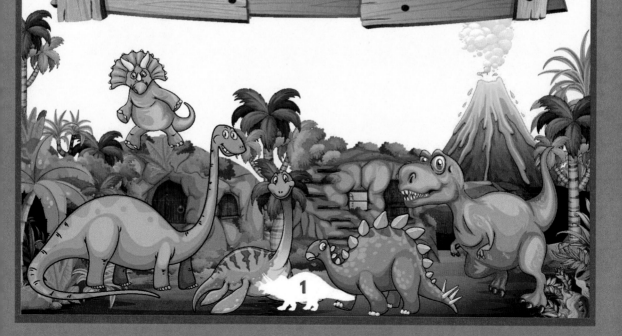

1

WHEN DID DINOSAURS LIVE?

The dinosaurs lived 180 million years ago during the mesozoic era. The Mesozoic era was split into three time periods named the Triassic, Jurassic and Cretaceous periods.

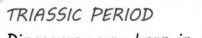

TRIASSIC PERIOD
Dinosaurs were born in this period.

JURASSIC PERIOD
Dinosaurs ruled the earth in this period.

CRETACEOUS PERIOD
Dinosaurs went extinct in this period.

A a

 Axe

 Apple

 Ape

AaAaAaAaAaAa

ALLOSAURUS

You should pronounce my name as "AL-oh-saw-russ".

My name means "other lizard".

I was found in Portugal & the U.S.A.

I was a carnivorous.

I was a large theropod.

I was 12 meters long.

Baby Rex is looking for her mommy! Can you help her?

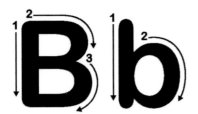

Ball

Boy

Bear

BbBb Bb Bb Bb Bb

BRACHIOSAURUS

You should pronounce my name as "BRAK-ee-oh-sore-us".

My name means "arm lizard".

I was found in Algeria, Portugal, Tanzania & the U.S.A.

I was a herbivore.

I was a sauropod.

I was 30 meters long.

Match the dinosaurs with the numbers

C c

Camp **Can** **Camel**

Cc Cc Cc Cc Cc

COELOPHYSIS

I was found in South Africa, the U.S.A & Zimbabwe.

I was a carnivore.

You should pronounce my name as "seel-OH-fie-sis".

I was a small theropod.

My name means "hollow form".

I was 2 meters long.

Draw the shapes in the empty space to *match the dinosaurs*

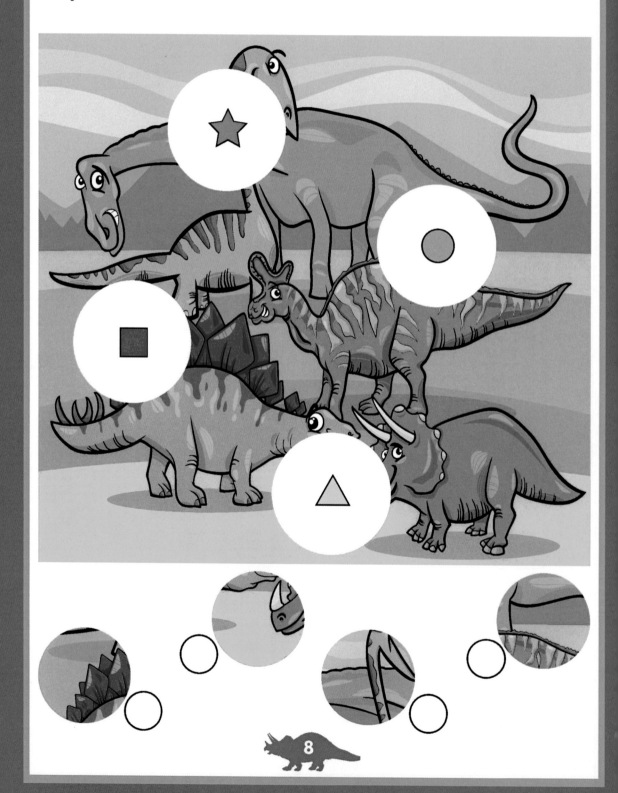

D d

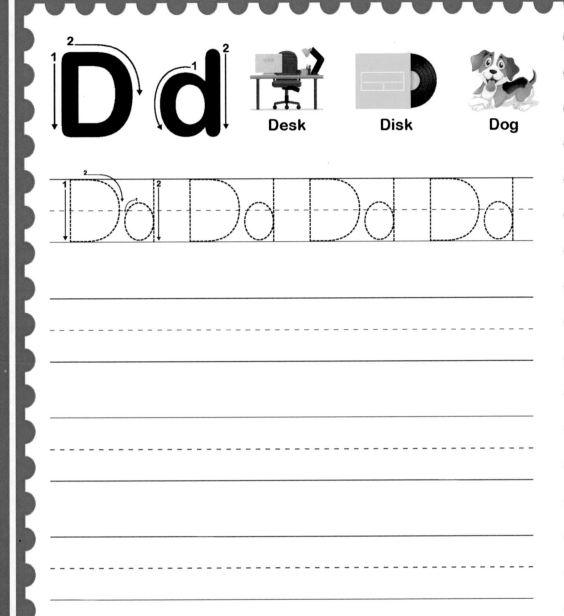

Desk　　**Disk**　　**Dog**

DIPLODOCUS

I was found in the U.S.A.

You should pronounce my name as "DIP-low DOCK-us".

I was a herbivore.

I was a sauropod.

My name means "double beam".

I was 26 meters long.

Color me!

E e

Ear

Europe

Elk

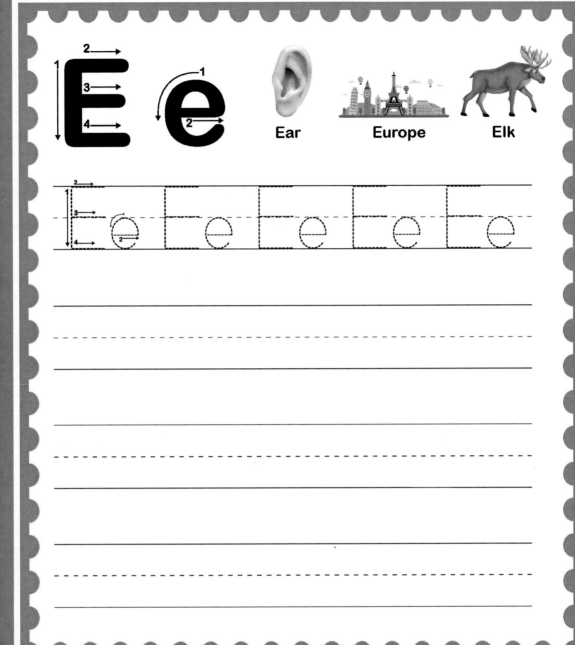

EDMONTOSAURUS

You should pronounce my name as "ed-MON-toe-sore-us".

My name means "Edmonton lizard".

I was found in Canada.

I was a herbivore.

I was an euornithopod.

I was 13 meters long.

HOW MANY DINOSAURS DO YOU SEE?

Write the answer here

ANSWER 8

F f

Fan

Fence

Fish

FABROSAURUS

You should pronounce my name as "FAB-ruh-SAWR-us".

My name means "True Reversed Vertebrae Lizard".

I was found in Africa & the U.S.A.

I was a herbivore.

I was an ornithischia.

I was 1 meters long.

Color me!

14

G g

Globe

Glue

Giraffe

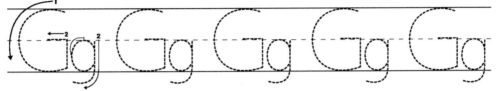

GIGANOTOSAURUS

I was found in Argentina.

You should pronounce my name as "gig-an-OH-toe-SORE-us".

I was a carnivore.

I was a large theropod.

My name means "giant southern lizard".

I was 12 meters long.

The mother dinosaur is looking for her eggs!

Can you help her?

16

Helicopter Hammer Hare

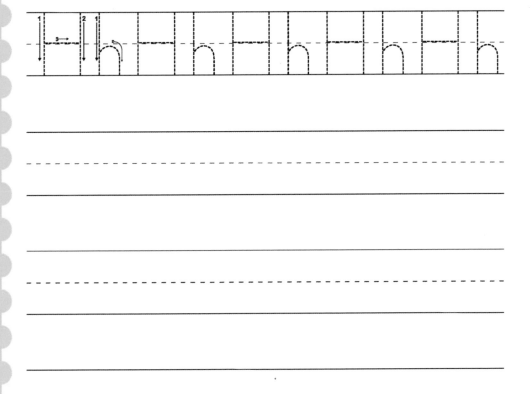

HYDROTHEROSAURUS

You should pronounce my name
as "Hy-dro-fee-roe-sore-us".

My name means
"water beast lizard".

I was found in the U.S.A.

I was a carnivore.

I was an elasmosaurus.

I was 13 meters long.

17

Color me!

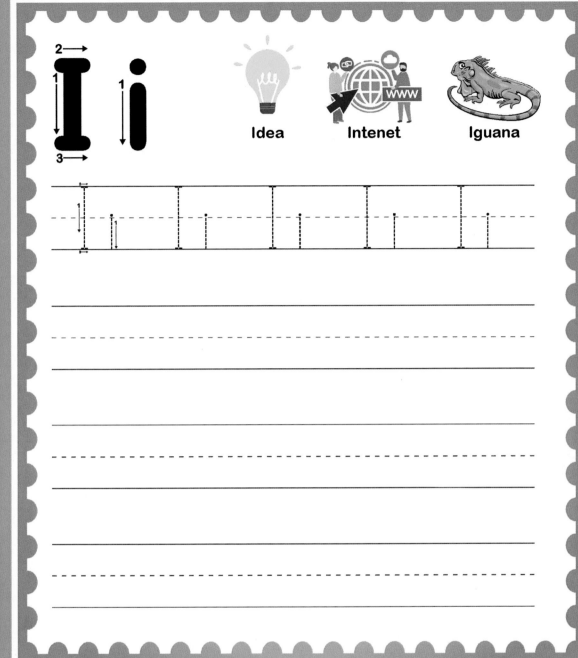

I i

Idea **Intenet** **Iguana**

IGUANODON

You should pronounce my name as "ig-WHA-noh-don".

My name means "iguana tooth".

I was found in Belgium, England & the U.S.A.

I was a herbivore.

I was an euornithopod.

I was 10 meters long.

Call a friend! Take out a dice and see who finishes first!

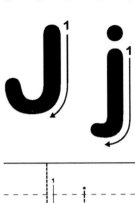

J j

Jewel

Jacket

Jaguar

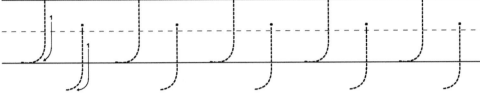

JANENSCHIA

You should pronounce my name as "yan-ensh-ee-ah".

I was named after "Janansch".

I was found in Tanzania.

I was a herbivore.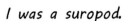

I was a suropod.

I was 20 meters long.

Match the mommy dinosaurs with the young ones

 ①  Ⓐ

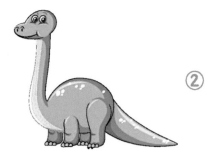 ②  Ⓑ

 ③  Ⓒ

 ④  Ⓓ

K k

Kite   Key   Kingfisher

K k K K K k K K K k K K K k

KENTROSAURUS

You should pronounce my name as "ken-TROH-sore-us."

My name means "spiky lizard."

I was found in Tanzania.

I was a herbivore.

I was an armoured dinosaur.

I was 5 meters long.

23

FIND 10 DIFFERENCES

Anwers

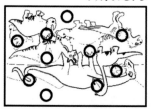

24

L l

Lake   Leave   Lion

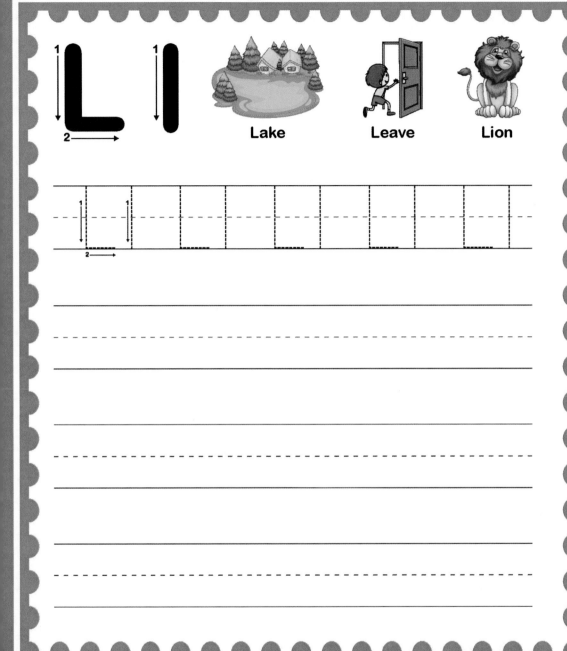

LAMBEOSAURUS

You should pronounce my name as "lam-BEE-oh-SORE-us".

My name means "Lambe's lizard".

I was found in Canada.

I was a herbivore.

I was an euornithopod.

I was 9 meters long.

Match our names correctly

 ● ● DIPLODOCUS

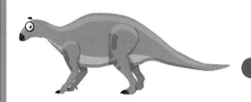 ● ● GIGANOTOSAURUS

 ● ● HYDROTHEROSAURUS

 ● ● IGUANODON

Magic

 Magnet

 Mouse

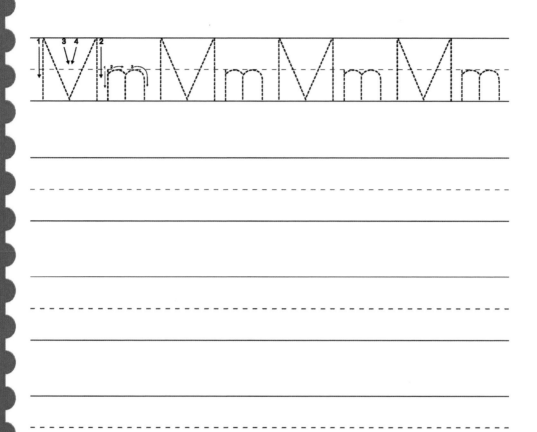

MASIAKASAURUS

You should pronounce my name
as "mah-shee-ah-kah-sore-us".

My name means
"vicious lizard".

I was found in Madagascar.

I was a carnivore.

I was a small theropod.

I was 2 meters long.

Number the rearranged parts

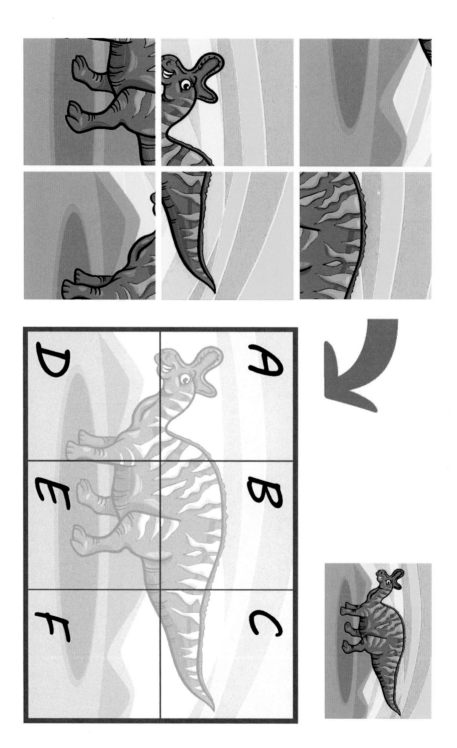

28

Notebook

Needle

Nightingale

$\mathcal{N}$ODOSAURUS

You should pronounce my name as "no-doh-SORE-us".

My name means "node lizard".

I was found in the U.S.A.

I was a herbivore.

I was an armoured dinosaur.

I was 5 meters long.

Classification of Dinosaurs

Theropods means "Beast foot". We only
ate meat and we had powerful claws
for hunting. Example:
Tyrannosaurus (T-Rex), Velociraptor

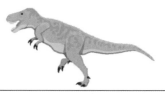

Sauropods means "lizard footed reptiles".
We had long necks; we walked on
four legs and we were herbivores.
Example: Brachiosaurus, Diplodocus

Thyreophora means roofed reptiles.
We were slow moving; we had spikes
or bony plates all over our body.
Example: Stegosaurs, Ankylosauria

Cerapods means horned face reptiles
We had horn filled heads,
birdlike beaks and we lived in herds.
Example: Triceratops, Styracosaurus

O o

Ocean **Oven** **Ox**

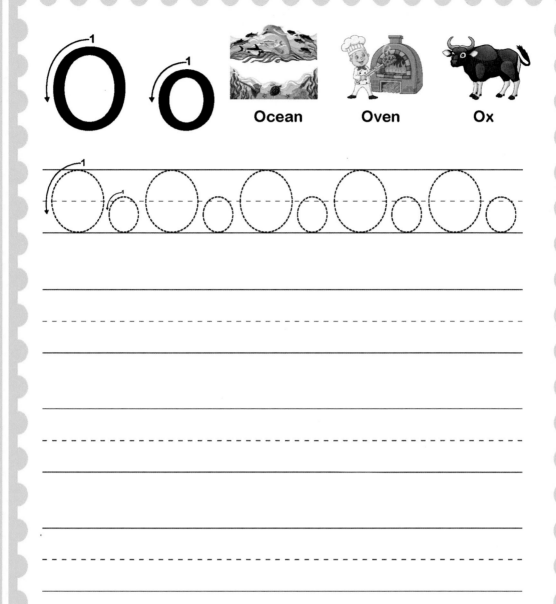

OVIRAPTOR

You should pronounce my name as "OH-vee-RAP-tor".

My name means "egg thief".

I was found in Mongolia.

I was an omnivore.

I was a small theropod.

I was 2 meters long.

Match the mommy dinosaurs with the young ones

 ① Ⓐ

 ② Ⓑ

 ③ Ⓒ

P p

Palace   Peas   Panda

P p   P p   P p   P p   P p

Color me!

34

Q q

Quiz Quartz Quail

Qq Qq Qq Qq

QUAESITOSAURUS

You should pronounce my name as "kwee-siet-oh-sore-us".

My name means "extraordinary lizard".

I was found in Mongolia.

I was a herbivore.

I was a sauropod.

I was 23 meters long.

Match the dinosaurs with the numbers

R r

Radish **Rain** **Raccoon**

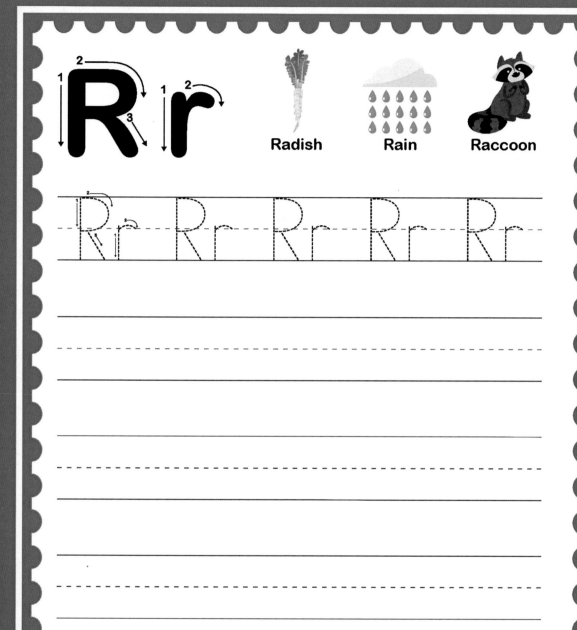

R r R r R r R r R r

RIOJASAURUS

You should pronounce my name as "ree-oh-hah-sore-us".

My name means "[La] Rioja lizard".

I was found in Argentina.

I was an omnivore.

I was a sauropod.

I was 5 meters long.

Here are some places where dinosaurs have been found:

1. The Badlands of South Dakota

2. Mongolia

3. The Hell Creek Formation, Montana

4. Manitoba, Canada

5. Death Valley, California

 **S** **s**

Satellite

Salt

Squirrel

Ss Ss Ss Ss Ss

𝓢PINOSAURUS

You should pronounce my name as "SPINE-oh-SORE-us".

My name means "thorn lizard".

I was found in Egypt & Morocco.

I was a carnivore.

I was a large theropod.

I was 18 meters long.

WHO DOES NOT FIT?

Circle me

T t

Train   **Tooth**   **Tiger**

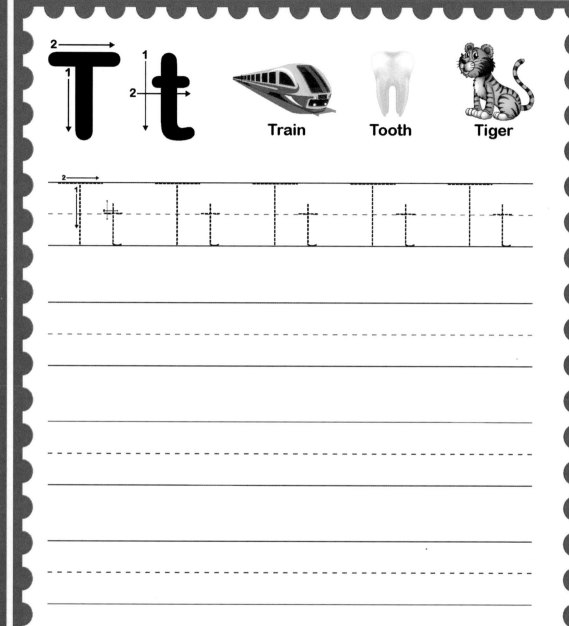

TYRANNOSAURUS

You should pronounce my name as "tie-RAN-oh-sore-us".

My name means "tyrant lizard".

I was found in Canada & the U.S.A.

I was a carnivore.

I was a large theropod.

I was 12 meters long.

Color me!

42

U u

Uniform

Utensils

Urial

UNENLAGIA

You should pronounce my name as "oon-en-lahg-ee-ah".

My name means "half bird".

I was found in Argentina.

I was a carnivore.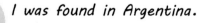

I was a small theropod.

I was 2 meters long.

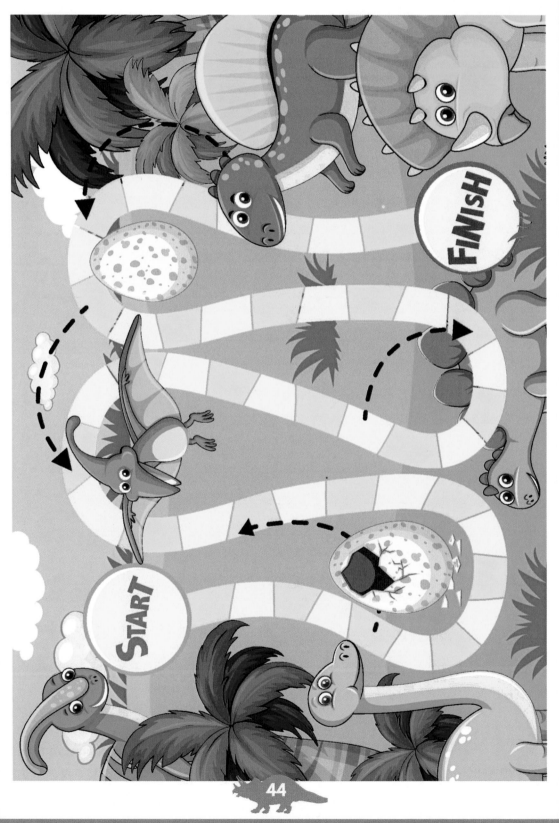

44

V v

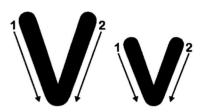 

 Volcano Violin  Vulture

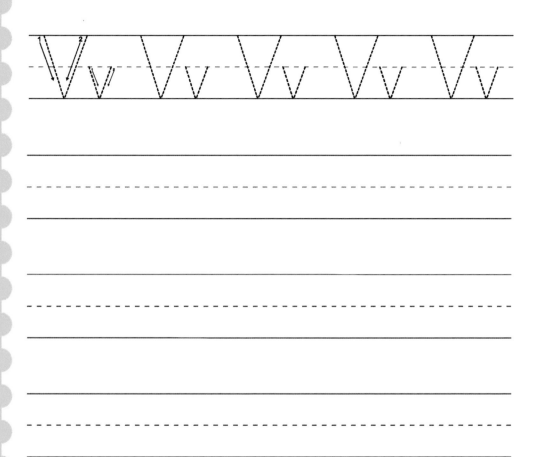

VELOCIRAPTOR

You should pronounce my name as "vel-OSS-ee-rap-tor".

My name means "quick plunderer".

I was found in Mongolia.

I was a carnivore.

I was a small theropod.

I was 2 meters long.

Color me!

Wall **Wagon** **Wolf**

WANNANOSAURUS

You should pronounce my name
as "wah-NAHN-uh-SAWR-us".

My name means
"Wannan Lizard".

I was found in China.

I was a herbivore.

I was an ornithischia.

I was 3 meters long.

47

Match the dinosaurs with the numbers

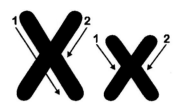

X-Ray

Xylophone

X-Ray Fish

Xiaosaurus

I was found in China.

You should pronounce my name as "Zhou-SAWR-us".

I was a herbivore.

I was an ornithischia.

My name means "Small Lizard".

I was 3 meters long.

Here are some museums where you can see dinosaur bones in real life!

Dinosaur National Monument - Colorado, Utah

Wyoming Dinosaur Center - Thermopolis, Wyoming

Dinosaur World - Plant City, Florida - Cave City, Kentucky - Glen Rose, Texas

The Academy of Natural Sciences - Philadelphia, Pennsylvania

Dinosaur State Park - Rocky Hill, Connecticut

The Field Museum - Chicago, Illinois

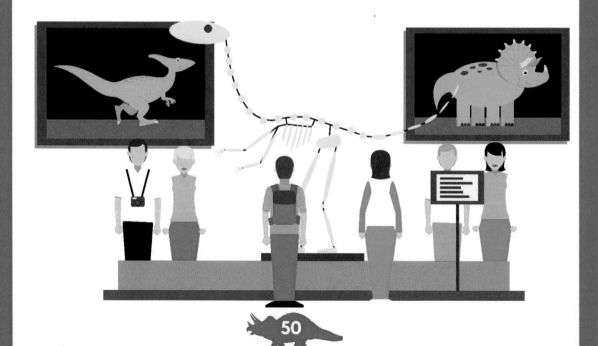

Y y

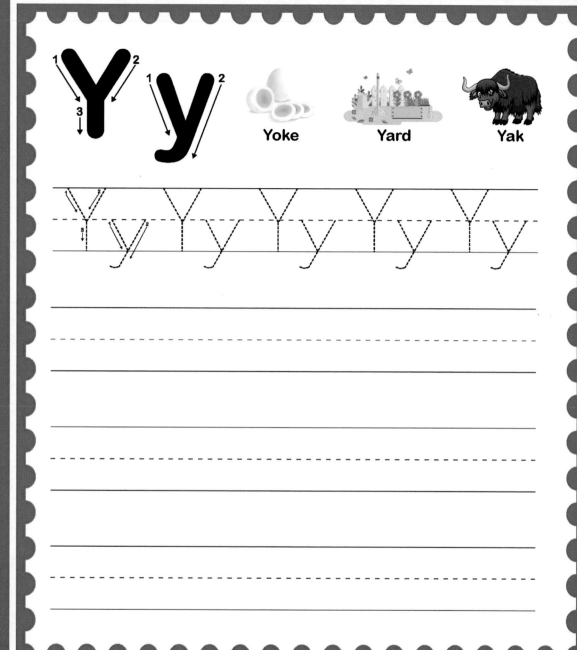

Yoke   **Yard**   **Yak**

YANGCHUANOSAURUS

You should pronounce my name as "yang-choo-AHN-oh-SORE-us".

My name means "Yangchuan lizard".

I was found in China.

I was a carnivore.

I was a large theropod.

I was 10 meters long.

Match the dinosaurs with right shadow

Z z

Zig Zag

Zoology

Zebra

ZUNICERATOPS

You should pronounce my
name as "zoo-nee-serra-tops".

My name means
"Zuni horned head".

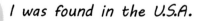
I was found in the U.S.A.

I was a herbivore.

I was a ceratopsian.

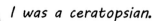
I was 10 meters long.

Match our names correctly

 ● ● BRACHIOSAURUS

 ● ● PARASAUROLOPHUS

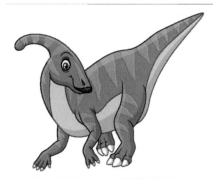 ● ● TYRANNOSAURUS

 ● ● VELOCIRAPTOR

LEARN THE ALPHABET
WITH DINOSAURS

www.aceacademicprep.com